this Notebook Belongs to:

____

By Adil Daisy

Monthly Budget

<table>
<tr><td colspan="3">INCOME</td></tr>
<tr><td>INCOME 1</td><td></td><td></td></tr>
<tr><td>INCOME 2</td><td></td><td></td></tr>
<tr><td>OTHER INCOME</td><td></td><td></td></tr>
<tr><td colspan="2">TOTAL INCOME</td><td></td></tr>
</table>

Expenses

Month:

$ Budget:

BIL TO BE PAID	DATE DUE	AMOUNT	PAID	NOTE

TOTAL

Monthly Budget

Other Expenses	Date	Amount	Note
Total			

Total Income

Total Expenses:

Diference

$ *Notes*

Monthly Budget

INCOME		
INCOME 1		
INCOME 2		
OTHER INCOME		
TOTAL INCOME		

Month:

$ Budget:

BIL TO BE PAID	DATE DUE	AMOUNT	PAID	NOTE
TOTAL				

Monthly Budget

Other Expenses	Date	Amount	Note
Total			

Total Income

Total Expenses:

Diference

$ *Notes*

Monthly Budget

INCOME		
INCOME 1		
INCOME 2		
OTHER INCOME		
TOTAL INCOME		

Expenses

Month:

$ Budget:

BIL TO BE PAID	DATE DUE	AMOUNT	PAID	NOTE

TOTAL

Monthly Budget

Other Expenses	Date	Amount	Note

Total

$ *Notes*

Total Income

Total Expenses:

Diference

Monthly Budget

Income

INCOME		
INCOME 1		
INCOME 2		
OTHER INCOME		
TOTAL INCOME		

Expenses

Month:

$ Budget:

BIL TO BE PAID	DATE DUE	AMOUNT	PAID	NOTE
TOTAL				

Monthly Budget

Other Expenses	Date	Amount	Note
Total			

Total Income

Total Expenses:

Diference

$ *Notes*

Monthly Budget

Income

Income		
Income 1		
Income 2		
Other Income		
Total Income		

Expenses

📅 **Month:**

💲 **Budget:**

Bil To Be Paid	Date Due	Amount	Paid	Note

Total

Monthly Budget

Other Expenses	Date	Amount	Note

Total

Total Income

Total Expenses:

Diference

$ *Notes*

Monthly Budget

Income

INCOME		
INCOME 1		
INCOME 2		
OTHER INCOME		
TOTAL INCOME		

Expenses

📅 **Month:**

💲 **Budget:**

BIL TO BE PAID	DATE DUE	AMOUNT	PAID	NOTE
TOTAL				

Monthly Budget

Other Expenses	Date	Amount	Note

Total

Total Income

Total Expenses:

Diference

$ *Notes*

Monthly Budget

Income

INCOME		
INCOME 1		
INCOME 2		
OTHER INCOME		
TOTAL INCOME		

Expenses

📅 **Month:**

💲 **Budget:**

BIL TO BE PAID	DATE DUE	AMOUNT	PAID	NOTE
TOTAL				

Monthly Budget

Other Expenses	Date	Amount	Note
Total			

Total Income

Total Expenses:

Diference

$ *Notes*

Monthly Budget

Income

Income		
Income 1		
Income 2		
Other Income		
Total Income		

Expenses

📅 **Month:**

💲 **Budget:**

Bil To Be Paid	Date Due	Amount	Paid	Note
Total				

Monthly Budget

Other Expenses	Date	Amount	Note

Total

Total Income

Total Expenses:

Diference

$ Notes

Monthly Budget

Income

INCOME		
INCOME 1		
INCOME 2		
OTHER INCOME		
TOTAL INCOME		

Expenses

📅 **Month:**

$ **Budget:**

BIL TO BE PAID	DATE DUE	AMOUNT	PAID	NOTE
TOTAL				

Monthly Budget

Other Expenses	Date	Amount	Note
Total			

Total Income

Total Expenses:

Diference

$ *Notes*

Monthly Budget

INCOME

INCOME		
INCOME 1		
INCOME 2		
OTHER INCOME		
TOTAL INCOME		

Expenses

📅 **Month:**

💲 **Budget:**

BIL TO BE PAID	DATE DUE	AMOUNT	PAID	NOTE

TOTAL

Monthly Budget

Other Expenses	Date	Amount	Note

Total

Total Income

Total Expenses:

Diference

$ Notes

Monthly Budget

INCOME		
INCOME 1		
INCOME 2		
OTHER INCOME		
TOTAL INCOME		

Expenses

Month:

$ Budget:

BIL TO BE PAID	DATE DUE	AMOUNT	PAID	NOTE

TOTAL

Monthly Budget

Other Expenses	Date	Amount	Note
Total			

Total Income

Total Expenses:

Diference

$ *Notes*

Monthly Budget

INCOME

INCOME 1		
INCOME 2		
OTHER INCOME		
TOTAL INCOME		

Expenses

📅 **Month:**

💲 **Budget:**

BIL TO BE PAID	DATE DUE	AMOUNT	PAID	NOTE

TOTAL

Monthly Budget

Other Expenses	Date	Amount	Note

Total

Total Income

Total Expenses:

Diference

$ *Notes*

Monday DATE: __________

DESCRIPTION	AMOUNT

tuesday DATE: __________

DESCRIPTION	AMOUNT

Wednesday DATE: __________

DESCRIPTION	AMOUNT

thursday DATE: __________

DESCRIPTION	AMOUNT

| $ | **TOTAL EXPENSES:** | **BALANCE:** |

Friday   DATE: __________

DESCRIPTION	AMOUNT

Saturday   DATE: __________

DESCRIPTION	AMOUNT

Sunday   DATE: __________

DESCRIPTION	AMOUNT

$ Notes

____
____
____
____
____
____
____
____
____

<table>
<tr><td>MONTH:</td><td>WEEK OFF:</td><td>BUDGET:</td></tr>
</table>

Monday DATE: __________

DESCRIPTION	AMOUNT

Tuesday DATE: __________

DESCRIPTION	AMOUNT

Wednesday DATE: __________

DESCRIPTION	AMOUNT

Thursday DATE: __________

DESCRIPTION	AMOUNT

$	**TOTAL EXPENSES:**		**BALANCE:**

Friday   DATE: _____________

DESCRIPTION	AMOUNT

Saturday   DATE: _____________

DESCRIPTION	AMOUNT

Sunday   DATE: _____________

DESCRIPTION	AMOUNT

$ Notes

Monday   DATE: __________

DESCRIPTION	AMOUNT

Tuesday   DATE: __________

DESCRIPTION	AMOUNT

Wednesday   DATE: __________

DESCRIPTION	AMOUNT

Thursday   DATE: __________

DESCRIPTION	AMOUNT

Friday

DATE: __________

DESCRIPTION	AMOUNT

Saturday

DATE: __________

DESCRIPTION	AMOUNT

Sunday

DATE: __________

DESCRIPTION	AMOUNT

$ Notes

____

____

____

____

____

____

____

____

<table>
<tr><td>MONTH:</td><td>WEEK OFF:</td><td>BUDGET:</td></tr>
</table>

Monday   DATE: __________

DESCRIPTION	AMOUNT

Tuesday   DATE: __________

DESCRIPTION	AMOUNT

Wednesday   DATE: __________

DESCRIPTION	AMOUNT

Thursday   DATE: __________

DESCRIPTION	AMOUNT

Friday   DATE: __________

DESCRIPTION	AMOUNT

Saturday   DATE: __________

DESCRIPTION	AMOUNT

Sunday   DATE: __________

DESCRIPTION	AMOUNT

$ Notes

____

____

____

____

____

____

____

____

<table>
<tr><td>MONTH:</td><td>WEEK OFF:</td><td>BUDGET:</td></tr>
</table>

Monday DATE: __________

Description	Amount

Tuesday DATE: __________

Description	Amount

Wednesday DATE: __________

Description	Amount

Thursday DATE: __________

Description	Amount

$ TOTAL EXPENSES:	BALANCE:

Friday DATE: __________

DESCRIPTION	AMOUNT

Saturday DATE: __________

DESCRIPTION	AMOUNT

Sunday DATE: __________

DESCRIPTION	AMOUNT

$ Notes

____

____

____

____

____

____

____

____

Monday   DATE: __________

DESCRIPTION	AMOUNT

tuesday   DATE: __________

DESCRIPTION	AMOUNT

Wednesday   DATE: __________

DESCRIPTION	AMOUNT

thursday   DATE: __________

DESCRIPTION	AMOUNT

$ TOTAL EXPENSES: | **BALANCE:**

Friday   DATE: __________

DESCRIPTION	AMOUNT

Saturday   DATE: __________

DESCRIPTION	AMOUNT

Sunday   DATE: __________

DESCRIPTION	AMOUNT

$ Notes

____

____

____

____

____

____

____

____

Monday DATE: __________

DESCRIPTION	AMOUNT

tuesday DATE: __________

DESCRIPTION	AMOUNT

Wednesday DATE: __________

DESCRIPTION	AMOUNT

Thursday DATE: __________

DESCRIPTION	AMOUNT

$ TOTAL EXPENSES: | **BALANCE:**

Friday

DATE: _____________

DESCRIPTION	AMOUNT

Saturday

DATE: _____________

DESCRIPTION	AMOUNT

Sunday

DATE: _____________

DESCRIPTION	AMOUNT

$ Notes

<table>
<tr><td>MONTH:</td><td>WEEK OFF:</td><td>BUDGET:</td></tr>
</table>

Monday   DATE: __________

DESCRIPTION	AMOUNT

tuesday   DATE: __________

DESCRIPTION	AMOUNT

Wednesday   DATE: __________

DESCRIPTION	AMOUNT

Thursday   DATE: __________

DESCRIPTION	AMOUNT

$ TOTAL EXPENSES:	BALANCE:

Friday DATE: _________

DESCRIPTION	AMOUNT

Saturday DATE: _________

DESCRIPTION	AMOUNT

Sunday DATE: _________

DESCRIPTION	AMOUNT

$ Notes

<table>
<tr><td>MONTH:</td><td>WEEK OFF:</td><td>BUDGET:</td></tr>
</table>

Monday   DATE: __________

DESCRIPTION	AMOUNT

tuesday   DATE: __________

DESCRIPTION	AMOUNT

Wednesday   DATE: __________

DESCRIPTION	AMOUNT

Thursday   DATE: __________

DESCRIPTION	AMOUNT

<table>
<tr><td> **TOTAL EXPENSES:**</td><td> **BALANCE:**</td></tr>
</table>

Friday DATE: __________

DESCRIPTION	AMOUNT

Saturday DATE: __________

DESCRIPTION	AMOUNT

Sunday DATE: __________

DESCRIPTION	AMOUNT

$ Notes

____

____

____

____

____

____

____

<table>
<tr><td>MONTH:</td><td>WEEK OFF:</td><td>BUDGET:</td></tr>
</table>

Monday   DATE: __________

DESCRIPTION	AMOUNT

tuesday   DATE: __________

DESCRIPTION	AMOUNT

Wednesday   DATE: __________

DESCRIPTION	AMOUNT

thursday   DATE: __________

DESCRIPTION	AMOUNT

TOTAL EXPENSES: **BALANCE:**

Friday   DATE: __________

DESCRIPTION	AMOUNT

Saturday   DATE: __________

DESCRIPTION	AMOUNT

Sunday   DATE: __________

DESCRIPTION	AMOUNT

Notes

____

____

____

____

____

____

____

<table>
<tr><td>MONTH:</td><td>WEEK OFF:</td><td>BUDGET:</td></tr>
</table>

Monday   DATE: __________

DESCRIPTION	AMOUNT

tuesday   DATE: __________

DESCRIPTION	AMOUNT

Wednesday   DATE: __________

DESCRIPTION	AMOUNT

thursday   DATE: __________

DESCRIPTION	AMOUNT

$	**TOTAL EXPENSES:**	◷ $	**BALANCE:**

Friday

DATE: __________

DESCRIPTION	AMOUNT

Saturday

DATE: __________

DESCRIPTION	AMOUNT

Sunday

DATE: __________

DESCRIPTION	AMOUNT

$ *Notes*

____

____

____

____

____

____

____

Monday   DATE: __________

DESCRIPTION	AMOUNT

tuesday   DATE: __________

DESCRIPTION	AMOUNT

Wednesday   DATE: __________

DESCRIPTION	AMOUNT

thursday   DATE: __________

DESCRIPTION	AMOUNT

$	**TOTAL EXPENSES:**	🕐$	**BALANCE:**

Friday

DATE: _____________

DESCRIPTION	AMOUNT

Saturday

DATE: _____________

DESCRIPTION	AMOUNT

Sunday

DATE: _____________

DESCRIPTION	AMOUNT

$ Notes

Monday   DATE: __________

DESCRIPTION	AMOUNT

tuesday   DATE: __________

DESCRIPTION	AMOUNT

Wednesday   DATE: __________

DESCRIPTION	AMOUNT

Thursday   DATE: __________

DESCRIPTION	AMOUNT

TOTAL EXPENSES:

BALANCE:

Friday

DATE: ___________

DESCRIPTION	AMOUNT

Saturday

DATE: ___________

DESCRIPTION	AMOUNT

Sunday

DATE: ___________

DESCRIPTION	AMOUNT

Notes

<table>
<tr><td>MONTH:</td><td>WEEK OFF:</td><td>BUDGET:</td></tr>
</table>

Monday   DATE: __________

DESCRIPTION	AMOUNT

tuesday   DATE: __________

DESCRIPTION	AMOUNT

Wednesday   DATE: __________

DESCRIPTION	AMOUNT

thursday   DATE: __________

DESCRIPTION	AMOUNT

$ TOTAL EXPENSES: **BALANCE:**

Friday   DATE: __________

DESCRIPTION	AMOUNT

Saturday   DATE: __________

DESCRIPTION	AMOUNT

Sunday   DATE: __________

DESCRIPTION	AMOUNT

$ Notes

____
____
____
____
____
____
____
____

<table>
<tr><td>MONTH:</td><td>WEEK OFF:</td><td>BUDGET:</td></tr>
</table>

Monday   DATE: __________

Description	Amount

tuesday   DATE: __________

Description	Amount

Wednesday   DATE: __________

Description	Amount

Thursday   DATE: __________

Description	Amount

Friday   DATE: _____________

DESCRIPTION	AMOUNT

Saturday   DATE: _____________

DESCRIPTION	AMOUNT

Sunday   DATE: _____________

DESCRIPTION	AMOUNT

$ Notes

<table>
<tr><td>MONTH:</td><td>WEEK OFF:</td><td>BUDGET:</td></tr>
</table>

Monday

DATE: _____________

DESCRIPTION	AMOUNT

tuesday

DATE: _____________

DESCRIPTION	AMOUNT

Wednesday

DATE: _____________

DESCRIPTION	AMOUNT

Thursday

DATE: _____________

DESCRIPTION	AMOUNT

$	**Total Expenses:**		**Balance:**

Friday Date: __________

Description	Amount

Saturday Date: __________

Description	Amount

Sunday Date: __________

Description	Amount

$ Notes

____

____

____

____

____

____

____

<table>
<tr><td>MONTH:</td><td>WEEK OFF:</td><td>BUDGET:</td></tr>
</table>

Monday   DATE: __________

DESCRIPTION	AMOUNT

tuesday   DATE: __________

DESCRIPTION	AMOUNT

Wednesday   DATE: __________

DESCRIPTION	AMOUNT

Thursday   DATE: __________

DESCRIPTION	AMOUNT

$ TOTAL EXPENSES: | **BALANCE:**

Friday   DATE: __________

DESCRIPTION	AMOUNT

Saturday   DATE: __________

DESCRIPTION	AMOUNT

Sunday   DATE: __________

DESCRIPTION	AMOUNT

$ Notes

____

____

____

____

____

____

____

____

Monday DATE: __________

DESCRIPTION	AMOUNT

tuesday DATE: __________

DESCRIPTION	AMOUNT

Wednesday DATE: __________

DESCRIPTION	AMOUNT

Thursday DATE: __________

DESCRIPTION	AMOUNT

$	**TOTAL EXPENSES:**	**BALANCE:**

Friday   DATE: _____________

DESCRIPTION	AMOUNT

Saturday   DATE: _____________

DESCRIPTION	AMOUNT

Sunday   DATE: _____________

DESCRIPTION	AMOUNT

$ Notes

____

____

____

____

____

____

____

<table>
<tr><td>MONTH:</td><td>WEEK OFF:</td><td>BUDGET:</td></tr>
</table>

Monday DATE: __________

DESCRIPTION	AMOUNT

tuesday DATE: __________

DESCRIPTION	AMOUNT

Wednesday DATE: __________

DESCRIPTION	AMOUNT

thursday DATE: __________

DESCRIPTION	AMOUNT

Friday   DATE: __________

DESCRIPTION	AMOUNT

Saturday   DATE: __________

DESCRIPTION	AMOUNT

Sunday   DATE: __________

DESCRIPTION	AMOUNT

$ Notes

____
____
____
____
____
____
____
____
____

<table>
<tr><td>MONTH:</td><td>WEEK OFF:</td><td>BUDGET:</td></tr>
</table>

Monday   DATE: __________

DESCRIPTION	AMOUNT

tuesday   DATE: __________

DESCRIPTION	AMOUNT

Wednesday   DATE: __________

DESCRIPTION	AMOUNT

thursday   DATE: __________

DESCRIPTION	AMOUNT

Friday   DATE: _____________

DESCRIPTION	AMOUNT

Saturday   DATE: _____________

DESCRIPTION	AMOUNT

Sunday   DATE: _____________

DESCRIPTION	AMOUNT

$ Notes

____

____

____

____

____

____

____

<table>
<tr><td>MONTH:</td><td>WEEK OFF:</td><td>BUDGET:</td></tr>
</table>

Monday — DATE: __________

DESCRIPTION	AMOUNT

Tuesday — DATE: __________

DESCRIPTION	AMOUNT

Wednesday — DATE: __________

DESCRIPTION	AMOUNT

Thursday — DATE: __________

DESCRIPTION	AMOUNT

 **TOTAL EXPENSES:** | **BALANCE:**

Friday   DATE: __________

DESCRIPTION	AMOUNT

Saturday   DATE: __________

DESCRIPTION	AMOUNT

Sunday   DATE: __________

DESCRIPTION	AMOUNT

Notes

<table>
<tr><td>MONTH:</td><td>WEEK OFF:</td><td>BUDGET:</td></tr>
</table>

Monday   DATE: __________

DESCRIPTION	AMOUNT

tuesday   DATE: __________

DESCRIPTION	AMOUNT

Wednesday   DATE: __________

DESCRIPTION	AMOUNT

thursday   DATE: __________

DESCRIPTION	AMOUNT

Friday DATE: __________

DESCRIPTION	AMOUNT

Saturday DATE: __________

DESCRIPTION	AMOUNT

Sunday DATE: __________

DESCRIPTION	AMOUNT

$ Notes

____

____

____

____

____

____

____

____

Monday

DATE: __________

DESCRIPTION	AMOUNT

tuesday

DATE: __________

DESCRIPTION	AMOUNT

Wednesday

DATE: __________

DESCRIPTION	AMOUNT

thursday

DATE: __________

DESCRIPTION	AMOUNT

$ TOTAL EXPENSES: | **BALANCE:**

Friday   DATE: __________

DESCRIPTION	AMOUNT

Saturday   DATE: __________

DESCRIPTION	AMOUNT

Sunday   DATE: __________

DESCRIPTION	AMOUNT

$ Notes

____
____
____
____
____
____
____
____

<table>
<tr><td>MONTH:</td><td>WEEK OFF:</td><td>BUDGET:</td></tr>
</table>

Monday   DATE: __________

DESCRIPTION	AMOUNT

tuesday   DATE: __________

DESCRIPTION	AMOUNT

Wednesday   DATE: __________

DESCRIPTION	AMOUNT

thursday   DATE: __________

DESCRIPTION	AMOUNT

| $ | **TOTAL EXPENSES:** | | **BALANCE:** |

Friday   DATE: __________

DESCRIPTION	AMOUNT

Saturday   DATE: __________

DESCRIPTION	AMOUNT

Sunday   DATE: __________

DESCRIPTION	AMOUNT

$ Notes

____
____
____
____
____
____
____
____
____

<table>
<tr><td>MONTH:</td><td>WEEK OFF:</td><td>BUDGET:</td></tr>
</table>

Monday   DATE: __________

DESCRIPTION	AMOUNT

Tuesday   DATE: __________

DESCRIPTION	AMOUNT

Wednesday   DATE: __________

DESCRIPTION	AMOUNT

Thursday   DATE: __________

DESCRIPTION	AMOUNT

Friday DATE: __________

DESCRIPTION	AMOUNT

Saturday DATE: __________

DESCRIPTION	AMOUNT

Sunday DATE: __________

DESCRIPTION	AMOUNT

$ Notes

Monday   DATE: __________

DESCRIPTION	AMOUNT

Tuesday   DATE: __________

DESCRIPTION	AMOUNT

Wednesday   DATE: __________

DESCRIPTION	AMOUNT

Thursday   DATE: __________

DESCRIPTION	AMOUNT

Friday   DATE: __________

DESCRIPTION	AMOUNT

Saturday   DATE: __________

DESCRIPTION	AMOUNT

Sunday   DATE: __________

DESCRIPTION	AMOUNT

$ Notes

____
____
____
____
____
____
____
____

<table>
<tr><td>MONTH:</td><td>WEEK OFF:</td><td>BUDGET:</td></tr>
</table>

Monday   DATE: __________

DESCRIPTION	AMOUNT

Tuesday   DATE: __________

DESCRIPTION	AMOUNT

Wednesday   DATE: __________

DESCRIPTION	AMOUNT

Thursday   DATE: __________

DESCRIPTION	AMOUNT

 **Total Expenses:** | **Balance:**

Friday   Date: __________

Description	Amount

Saturday   Date: __________

Description	Amount

Sunday   Date: __________

Description	Amount

Notes

____

____

____

____

____

____

____

____

<table>
<tr><td>MONTH:</td><td>WEEK OFF:</td><td>BUDGET:</td></tr>
</table>

Monday   DATE: __________

DESCRIPTION	AMOUNT

tuesday   DATE: __________

DESCRIPTION	AMOUNT

Wednesday   DATE: __________

DESCRIPTION	AMOUNT

Thursday   DATE: __________

DESCRIPTION	AMOUNT

$ **TOTAL EXPENSES:**	**BALANCE:**

Friday   DATE: ___________

DESCRIPTION	AMOUNT

Saturday   DATE: ___________

DESCRIPTION	AMOUNT

Sunday   DATE: ___________

DESCRIPTION	AMOUNT

$ Notes

____

____

____

____

____

____

____

<table>
<tr><td>Month:</td><td>Week Off:</td><td>Budget:</td></tr>
</table>

Monday DATE: __________

Description	Amount

tuesday DATE: __________

Description	Amount

Wednesday DATE: __________

Description	Amount

Thursday DATE: __________

Description	Amount

$	**Total Expenses:**	**Balance:**

Friday

Date: __________

Description	Amount

Saturday

Date: __________

Description	Amount

Sunday

Date: __________

Description	Amount

Notes

____
____
____
____
____
____
____

<table>
<tr><td>MONTH:</td><td>WEEK OFF:</td><td>BUDGET:</td></tr>
</table>

Monday DATE: __________

DESCRIPTION	AMOUNT

tuesday DATE: __________

DESCRIPTION	AMOUNT

Wednesday DATE: __________

DESCRIPTION	AMOUNT

thursday DATE: __________

DESCRIPTION	AMOUNT

<table>
<tr><td>$ **TOTAL EXPENSES:**</td><td> $ **BALANCE:**</td></tr>
</table>

Friday   DATE: _________

DESCRIPTION	AMOUNT

Saturday   DATE: _________

DESCRIPTION	AMOUNT

Sunday   DATE: _________

DESCRIPTION	AMOUNT

$ Notes

____

____

____

____

____

____

____

Monday   DATE: __________

DESCRIPTION	AMOUNT

tuesday   DATE: __________

DESCRIPTION	AMOUNT

Wednesday   DATE: __________

DESCRIPTION	AMOUNT

Thursday   DATE: __________

DESCRIPTION	AMOUNT

Friday

DATE: __________

DESCRIPTION	AMOUNT

Saturday

DATE: __________

DESCRIPTION	AMOUNT

Sunday

DATE: __________

DESCRIPTION	AMOUNT

$ Notes

____
____
____
____
____
____
____
____

<table>
<tr><td>MONTH:</td><td>WEEK OFF:</td><td>BUDGET:</td></tr>
</table>

Monday   DATE: __________

DESCRIPTION	AMOUNT

tuesday   DATE: __________

DESCRIPTION	AMOUNT

Wednesday   DATE: __________

DESCRIPTION	AMOUNT

Thursday   DATE: __________

DESCRIPTION	AMOUNT

Friday   DATE: __________

DESCRIPTION	AMOUNT

Saturday   DATE: __________

DESCRIPTION	AMOUNT

Sunday   DATE: __________

DESCRIPTION	AMOUNT

$ Notes

____

____

____

____

____

____

____

<table>
<tr><td>MONTH:</td><td>WEEK OFF:</td><td>BUDGET:</td></tr>
</table>

Monday DATE: __________

DESCRIPTION	AMOUNT

tuesday DATE: __________

DESCRIPTION	AMOUNT

Wednesday DATE: __________

DESCRIPTION	AMOUNT

Thursday DATE: __________

DESCRIPTION	AMOUNT

$	**TOTAL EXPENSES:**	**BALANCE:**

Friday   DATE: __________

DESCRIPTION	AMOUNT

Saturday   DATE: __________

DESCRIPTION	AMOUNT

Sunday   DATE: __________

DESCRIPTION	AMOUNT

$ Notes

____

____

____

____

____

____

____

<table>
<tr><td>MONTH:</td><td>WEEK OFF:</td><td>BUDGET:</td></tr>
</table>

Monday   DATE: __________

DESCRIPTION	AMOUNT

tuesday   DATE: __________

DESCRIPTION	AMOUNT

Wednesday   DATE: __________

DESCRIPTION	AMOUNT

Thursday   DATE: __________

DESCRIPTION	AMOUNT

$	**Total Expenses:**	**Balance:**

Friday   Date: ___________

Description	Amount

Saturday   Date: ___________

Description	Amount

Sunday   Date: ___________

Description	Amount

$ Notes

____
____
____
____
____
____
____
____

Monday   DATE: __________

DESCRIPTION	AMOUNT

tuesday   DATE: __________

DESCRIPTION	AMOUNT

Wednesday   DATE: __________

DESCRIPTION	AMOUNT

thursday   DATE: __________

DESCRIPTION	AMOUNT

Friday   DATE: __________

DESCRIPTION	AMOUNT

Saturday   DATE: __________

DESCRIPTION	AMOUNT

Sunday   DATE: __________

DESCRIPTION	AMOUNT

$ Notes

____
____
____
____
____
____
____

<table>
<tr><td>MONTH:</td><td>WEEK OFF:</td><td>BUDGET:</td></tr>
</table>

Monday DATE: __________

DESCRIPTION	AMOUNT

Tuesday DATE: __________

DESCRIPTION	AMOUNT

Wednesday DATE: __________

DESCRIPTION	AMOUNT

Thursday DATE: __________

DESCRIPTION	AMOUNT

 **TOTAL EXPENSES:**

BALANCE:

Friday

DATE: _____________

DESCRIPTION	AMOUNT

Saturday

DATE: _____________

DESCRIPTION	AMOUNT

Sunday

DATE: _____________

DESCRIPTION	AMOUNT

Notes

____

____

____

____

____

____

____

____

Thank You!

We hope you enjoyed our Planner.

.

As a small familly company, your feedback is verry important to us.

Please let us know how you like our book at:

adildaisy@gmail.com

Printed in the USA
CPSIA information can be obtained
at www.ICGtesting.com
CBHW080527240724
12047CB00018B/585